Editor
Sara Connolly

Illustrator
Kevin McCarthy

Cover Artist
Denise Bauer

Editor in Chief
Ina Massler Levin, M.A.

Creative Director
Karen J. Goldfluss, M.S. Ed.

Art Coordinator
Renée Christine Yates

Imaging
James Edward Grace

Publisher
Mary D. Smith, M.S. Ed.

Paragraphs to Essays

Includes Standards & Benchmarks

Learn to organize and structure an essay.

Develop nonfiction writing skills.

Discover how to write for a specific audience.

Explore purpose for writing an essay.

One of the best parts about going camping eeping in a tent. It's good to set up the tent our first get to camp. Find a level area and clear any rocks or pine cones away. Make sure the tent site is away from a fire pit. Spread out a ground cover if you have one.

Author

Tracie I. Heskett M.Ed.

The classroom teacher may reproduce the materials in this book and/or CD for use in a single classroom only. The reproduction of any part of this book and/or CD for other classrooms or for an entire school or school system is strictly prohibited. No part of this publication may be transmitted or recorded in any form without written permission from the publisher with the exception of electronic material, which may be stored on the purchaser's computer only.

Teacher Created Resources, Inc.
12621 Western Avenue
Garden Grove, CA 92841
www.teachercreated.com

ISBN: 978-1-4206-3251-4

©2010 Teacher Created Resources, Inc.
Reprinted, 2016
Made in U.S.A.

Table of Contents

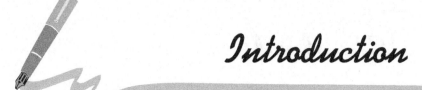

Introduction

When writing is considered an important component of the reading process, amazing things can happen. Writing, after all, is the expression of things learned. It is an active process when students are allowed to discover, reflect, and create. Higher order thinking skills are awakened as students analyze, synthesize, construct meaning and make connections through use of the written word. Research has shown that reading and writing are co-dependent, and the relationship thereof is that one cannot exist to full potential without the other; both reading and writing facilitate the other.

In order for students to benefit from the writing process, effective writing strategies should be introduced and practiced. Writing strategies will allow students to expand the natural thinking process and transform that thinking into the written word.

Paragraphs to Essays provides students with the opportunity to develop nonfiction writing skills. Lessons introduce students to specific types of writing, such as expository and expressive compositions. Originally, the word *essay* meant to try or to attempt. Michel de Montaigne defined his writing as "essays," saying that it was an attempt to put his thoughts down on paper. In that sense, any time a student writes a journal entry, it is a form of essay. Therefore, as students progress through the beginning steps of learning how to write an essay, several lessons will incorporate journal writing as an exercise.

Reading samples and observing models help students learn key components of an essay, such as an introduction, body paragraphs, and a conclusion. Students learn how to outline and incorporate details and examples to go with a main idea. They continue to develop paragraph writing skills as they compose practice essays, then edit them and prepare them for publication.

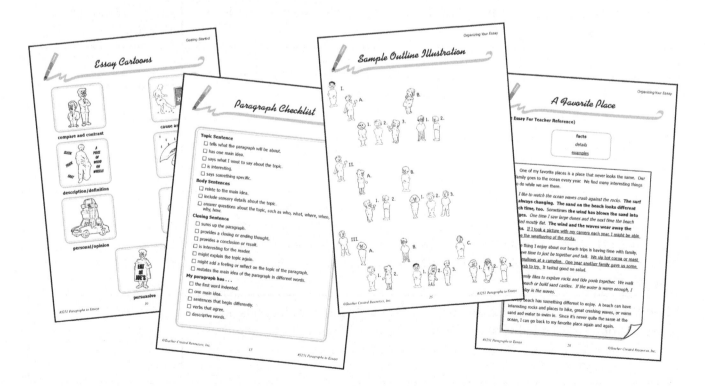

Standards

The lessons in *Paragraphs to Essays* meet the following writing standards, which are used with permission from McREL.

McREL, Mid–continent Research for Education and Learning, ©2009. Web site: **http://www.mcrel.org**
Telephone: (303) 337–0990

Standard	Pages
Standard 1 Uses the general skills and strategies of the writing process	
1.1 Uses prewriting strategies to plan written work (e.g., uses graphic organizers; groups related ideas; brainstorms ideas; organizes information according to type and purpose of writing)	6–7, 13, 23–26, 27–29, 38, 42–45
1.2 Uses strategies to draft and revise written work (e.g., elaborates on a central idea; writes with attention to audience, word choice, sentence variation; uses paragraphs to develop separate ideas)	13, 14–16, 17–18, 27–29, 32–34
1.3 Uses strategies to edit and publish written work (e.g., edits for grammar, punctuation, capitalization, and spelling at a developmentally appropriate level; considers page format (paragraphs, margins, indentations, titles)	47–48
1.4 Evaluates own and others' writing (e.g., determines the best features of a piece of writing; determines how writing achieves its purposes; responds to classmates' writing)	14–16, 19–20, 30–31, 35–37, 42–44, 46, 47–48
1.5 Uses strategies (e.g., determines knowledge and interests of audience) to write for different audiences (e.g., self, teachers)	14–16, 17–18
1.6 Uses strategies (e.g., adapts focus, determines knowledge and interests of audience) to write for a variety of purposes (e.g., to inform, entertain, explain, describe, record ideas)	19–20, 30–31
1.7 Writes expository compositions (e.g., identifies and stays on the topic; develops the topic with simple facts, details, examples, and explanations; excludes extraneous and inappropriate information; uses structures such as cause–and–effect, similarities and differences; provides a concluding statement)	8–11, 17–18, 23–26, 32–34, 35–37, 38, 39–41, 42–44
1.10 Writes expressive compositions (e.g., expresses ideas, reflections and observations; uses an individual, authentic voice; uses narrative strategies, relevant details, and ideas that enable the reader to imagine the world of the event or experience)	6–7, 13, 27–29, 46

Standard	Pages
1.11 Writes in response to literature (e.g., summarizes main ideas and significant details; relates own ideas to supporting details; advances judgments; supports judgments with references to the text, other works, other authors, non–print media, and personal knowledge	46
Standard 2. Uses the stylistic and rhetorical aspects of writing	
2.1 Uses descriptive language that clarifies and enhances ideas (e.g., common figures of speech, sensory details)	27–29, 38
2.2 Uses paragraph form in writing (e.g., indents the first word of a paragraph, uses topic sentences, recognizes a paragraph as a group of sentences about one main idea, uses an introductory and concluding paragraph)	14–16, 19–20, 30–31, 35–37, 38
Standard 4. Gathers and uses information for research purposes	21–22

What Is an Essay?

Objective

Students will experience what "essay" means as they learn definitions and express their understanding by completing pages for a class book.

Materials

- "A Piece of Your Mind" essay definitions, page 7
- whiteboard or overhead projector and appropriate markers

Preparation

Prepare essay definitions for classroom display. Label definitions. (optional)

Opening

1. Write the word *essay* on the board or overhead transparency. Review the guidelines for free writing:
   - Write without stopping.
   - Don't edit.
   - Write something—anything—so long as you keep writing.
2. Invite students to free write for two or three minutes about the word *essay*.

Directions

1. Refer to "A Piece of Your Mind" and read aloud (and post if desired) the definitions of essay.
2. Tell students they will "act out" the following quotation as they participate in this lesson.

   "Writing is a way to end up thinking something you couldn't have started out thinking…. At the end you see things differently." (P. Elbow)

3. Divide students into groups of three or four students each.
4. Have students discuss the definitions presented in class and their free writing from the Opening activity. You may wish to have students address the following questions:
   - Would all of the definitions apply to every essay? Why or why not?
   - Which things would every essay have to include?
   - Which aspects of an essay might not always be included?

Closing

1. Have students participate in another free writing session in which they explore how their understanding of *essay* has changed.
2. Ask students how they acted out the quotation. (*They started out with some ideas about essays, discussed with others, and considered how their thoughts changed.*)
3. Have students use their second free writing piece to create a page for a class book.
4. Compile, bind, or display student pages for reference as they learn to write essays.

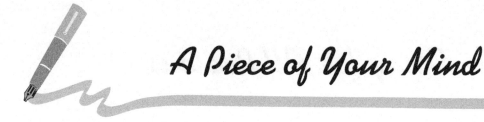

A Piece of Your Mind

An Essay...

- is a short composition that analyzes, interprets, or reflects on a topic.

- expresses an author's perspective or opinion on a topic and includes personality.

- states your personal point of view.

- is a "piece of your mind" that can be funny or serious.

- states what you think about a subject.

- might include research or quotes from others.

- can be a letter to the editor.

- grabs your attention.

- focuses on one aspect of a topic, perhaps the highlight.

An Essay for All Reasons

Objective

Students will correctly identify types of sample essays.

Materials

- "Types of Essays," page 9, for teacher reference
- "Essay Cartoons," page 10
- "Which One Am I?," pages 11–12, sample essay paragraphs of each type (Reading Levels: #1: 3.3; #2: 3.9; #3: 5.0; #4: 3.2; #5: 4.4; #6: 2.7; #7: 2.5)
- interactive whiteboard, chart paper, or overhead projector and appropriate markers

Opening

1. Have two or three volunteers review and explain the concept of an essay.
2. Display cartoon figures to introduce different types of essays.

Directions

1. Go over each type of essay in more detail. Use an interactive whiteboard, chart paper, or overhead transparency to take notes as a class. List a few characteristics students could use to identify each type of essay.

   - compare and contrast
   - cause and effect
   - description/definition
   - factual/informative
   - personal/opinion

2. Distribute copies of "Which One Am I?" (sample essay paragraphs).
3. Display cartoon figures for student reference. Have students write the type of essay next to each paragraph.
4. Go over student responses together as a class. Ask students how they arrived at their answers for each type of paragraph.

Closing

1. Ask students to choose one type of essay they would like to write. Have them draw their own cartoon characters representing that type of essay, explaining why they would like to write it.

 ©Teacher Created Resources, Inc.

Types of Essays

Compare and Contrast

In this type of essay, the writer describes similarities and differences between two items, ideas, or events.

Cause and Effect

The writer explores why things happen (causes) and the results (effects). The essay discusses an event or condition and the end result, or influence, it had on someone or something.

Description/Definition

The writer uses observations and detailed descriptions to create an experience for the reader. Students may write about a special person, place, or thing.

Factual/Informative

In this type of essay, the author gives information and explains something to the reader. It has facts rather than opinions.

Personal/Opinion

Include your own ideas and feelings about a topic. Include sensory details and explain why the event or experience is important.

Process

A process essay describes a series of actions taken to accomplish a specific task. Someone might write this type of essay to show another person how to do something.

Persuasive

In a persuasive essay, the author tries to convince the reader to do something or to change how he or she thinks or feels about a topic.

Essay Cartoons

compare and contrast

cause and effect

SLEEK
TRICK
FAST
A PIECE OF WOOD ON WHEELS

description/definition

IT'S RAINING!

factual

personal/opinion

process

EAT at JOE'S

persuasive

Which One Am I?

Directions:

On the lines provided, identify which kind of essay each example is.

#1—By K.M.

My favorite pet is a hamster because of its appearance and how it acts. My hamster is brown with white spots. A hamster looks cute when it cleans its face. Usually a hamster doesn't know when you caress it.

If you like adventurous pets, get a hamster. It runs around in a ball and finds out almost more about the house than you know! My hamster quickly scoots around the house in her ball. She also runs in her wheel very fast. If I wake up in the middle of the night, I can hear her spinning the wheel.

Hamsters have great personalities. They look at you when you talk to them. They don't get hurt easily if you take care of them.

Which one am I? _____

#2—by B.K.

Cowboys today do not do things the same as they did a long time ago. Cowboys work with horses and cows, but they have different equipment and machines to help them. Cowboys still ride horses. Now they use trailers and trucks to move cows.

Which one am I? _____

#3—by R.C.

Whenever you ride your bicycle to school, you should lock it up. Remember to bring something long enough to go through the frame of the bicycle, the tire, and the bike rack to which you want to lock it. If your lock has a key, keep the key in a safe place. If you lock your bike, no one can take it. It also shows you are responsible and take care of your possessions. Locking a bicycle discourages the wrong people from hanging out by the school trying to take things from students. It's just a good idea to lock your bike!

Which one am I? _____

#4—by S.R.

A mother chimpanzee teaches her youngster to hunt for termites. The mother strips a twig of its bark and puts the twig in a hole in the termite mound. Then she waits for quite awhile. She takes out the twig and quickly sucks the termites off.

Termites are not the only thing that chimpanzees eat. They also eat bark and berries. Sometimes they hunt down a deer for meat. Chimpanzees also eat honey, seeds, and insects. When they need a drink of water, they chew a wad of leaves and put the wad in tree holes. Then they take the leaves out and suck out the water.

Which one am I? _____

Which One Am I? (cont.)

#5—by K.M

The United States Army built many dams. Bonneville Dam spans the Columbia River. It lies between Oregon and Washington states. It makes electricity. This means people do not have to burn coal for power. Water power does not pollute the air. The dam protects the lowlands from flooding. People used to grow crops on the lowlands. Now there are buildings and houses. When the army built the dam, they had to cut down many trees. The dam flooded native fishing areas.

Which one am I? _____

#6 —by C.P.

One of the best parts about going camping is sleeping in a tent. It's good to set up the tent when you first get to camp. Find a level area and clear any rocks or pine cones away. Make sure the tent site is away from the fire pit. Spread out a ground cover if you have one. Then lay the tent out flat. Pound the four corner stakes into the ground. Then assemble the poles and thread them through the loops on the outside of the tent. It may take two people to raise one or more poles at the same time. Anchor the poles to the tent if it has ties or clips. Put any additional stakes in the tent around the sides. Finally, if you have a rain fly, put that over the top of the tent. Then you can enjoy sleeping in a warm, dry tent!

Which one am I? _____

#7—by J.G.

Our city park is a unique place. It has massive sycamore trees that have their own scent in the summer. A creek meanders through the park. I like to wade in the creek or just sit on the bank and watch it. Sometimes we build a small dam with rocks and sticks. Where the creek goes around a bend the water is deep enough to swim. I enjoy spending time in the park!

Which one am I? _____

- -

Answer Key

#1—personal, #2—compare/contrast, #3—persuasive, #4—factual/informative, #5—cause and effect, #6—process, #7—description/definition

Focus on a Topic

Objective

Students will explore essay topics by participating in a class activity and writing journal entries.

Materials

- interactive whiteboard, chart paper, or overhead projector and appropriate markers
- highlighters or colored pencils
- beanbag

Opening

1. As a class, brainstorm and choose a topic for a possible essay. Create a list of topics for student reference, for example:

   - why a particular event happened in your town or state history (cause and effect)
   - the similarities and differences between eating a hamburger at home or at a restaurant (compare/contrast)
   - a popular sport (description/definition)
   - an event coming up at school or in the community (factual/informative)
   - why students like their school or a particular subject (personal)
   - how to play a computer game (process)

2. Choose one topic for the activity. Try to state the topic as specifically as possible.

3. Have students stand in a circle. Students will take turns tossing a beanbag to one another. As each person catches the beanbag, he or she will say something about the chosen topic. Keep the activity moving and ensure as many students as possible have a turn.

Directions

1. Use the whiteboard, overhead transparency, or chart paper to take notes on the ideas students generated during the Opening activity.

2. Discuss the concept of focusing on a topic. Explain this is what the class did when they thought of different things about one topic.

3. Review the meaning of *explore*. (*to find out something new or discover something new about a place (or thing); to think about an idea carefully*)

4. Have students "explore" the topic further by writing a journal entry about it.

Closing

1. Have students use highlighters or colored pencils to underline specific statements in their writing about the topic.

2. Ask several students to share one or two examples of how they focused on the stated topic.

Paragraphs: The Building Blocks

Objective

Students will review how to write a complete paragraph.

Materials

- class-generated list of topics from "Focus on a Topic" lesson
- "Star Pattern," page 16, one copy per student and one copy for display
- cardstock

Preparation

1. Enlarge and photocopy the star pattern onto cardstock. Cut the star points apart.
2. Copy the bulleted list created in the Closing discussion for display if desired.

Opening

1. Ask students to describe how to write a complete paragraph.
2. Use the points of the star to demonstrate how all the sentences fit together and what information students might include in the body sentences of a paragraph.

Directions

1. Ask students to write a letter to a classmate describing how to write a paragraph. (Randomly assign names or instruct students to address their letters, "Dear Classmate.")
2. Collect student letters. Redistribute randomly so each student has a classmate's letter.
3. Have students follow the instructions in the letter they received to write a paragraph. You may wish to have students choose a topic from the class-generated list, write about a subject of current study (in science or social studies, for example), or write about a topic of interest to them.
4. Collect student paragraphs. You may also wish to collect student letters for your assessment of student understanding.

Closing

1. As a class, review what makes a strong paragraph.
2. Create a checklist similar to the one on the following page.
3. Cover or remove names on student paragraphs and redistribute so each student has a classmate's paragraph.
4. Have students refer to the checklist to read and evaluate their classmates' paragraphs. You may wish to have students rate the paragraphs by drawing a number of stars at the top of the page, indicating the writing is a "three-star" or a "four-star" paragraph, for example.

Paragraph Checklist

Topic Sentence

☐ tells what the paragraph will be about.

☐ has one main idea.

☐ says what I want to say about the topic.

☐ is interesting.

☐ says something specific.

Body Sentences

☐ relate to the main idea.

☐ include sensory details about the topic.

☐ answer questions about the topic, such as who, what, where, when, why, how.

Closing Sentence

☐ sums up the paragraph.

☐ provides a closing or ending thought.

☐ provides a conclusion or result.

☐ is interesting for the reader.

☐ might explain the topic again.

☐ might add a feeling or reflect on the topic of the paragraph.

☐ restates the main idea of the paragraph in different words.

My paragraph has . . .

☐ the first word indented.

☐ one main idea.

☐ sentences that begin differently.

☐ verbs that agree.

☐ descriptive words.

Star Pattern

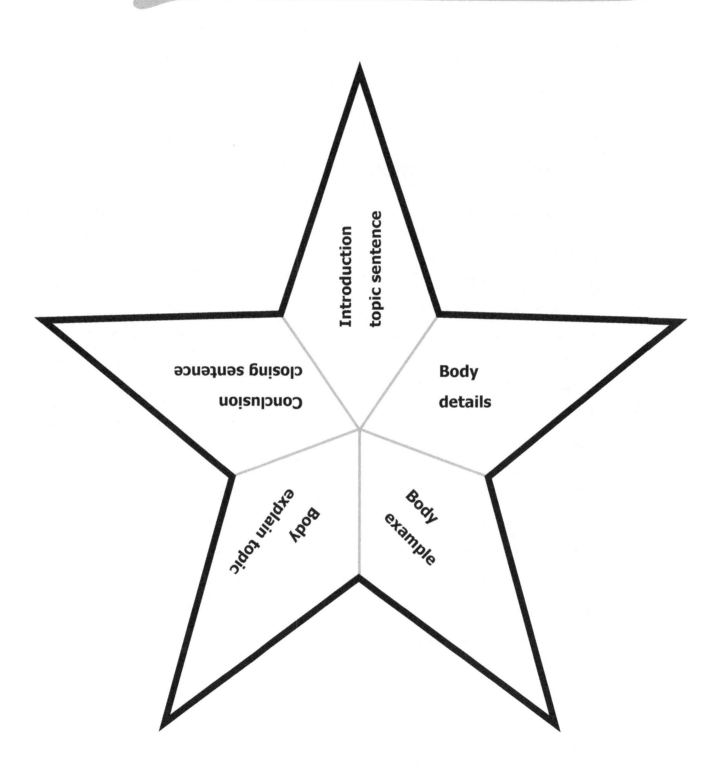

Introduction
topic sentence

Body
details

Body
example

Body
explain topic

Conclusion
closing sentence

16

©Teacher Created Resources, Inc.

Know Your Audience

Objective

Students will review the types of essays, consider various groups of people who might read their writing, select a topic and target audience, and write brief essays.

Materials

- "Essay Cartoons," page 10
- interactive whiteboard or chart paper and appropriate markers
- magazine pictures of people

Preparation

Number the cartoon figures.

Opening

1. Display the cartoon figures. Ask students to list groups of people who might want to read each type of essay.

2. Help students think of broad categories of people, such as:
   - someone who needs the information (factual)
   - someone who likes or is interested in the topic being described (description/definition)
   - someone who wants to understand why something happened or what caused it (cause and effect)
   - someone who wants to make a choice between two options (compare/contrast, persuasive)
   - someone who wants to know how people feel about a topic or issue (personal, opinion)

3. Match each cartoon figure (type of essay) to a category of reader.

Directions

1. Discuss the different groups of people who might want to read student essays.

2. Create a class chart listing various groups of people, similar to the one shown below.

peers	teachers	family members	other grownups	younger students/ siblings

3. Use an interactive whiteboard to ensure each student has a copy or have students copy the chart from the board.

Know Your Audience (cont.)

Directions (cont.)

4. Have students use the list of types of essays (see cartoon figures for review) and student-generated list of possible topics created in the "Focus on a Topic" lesson to select one topic to consider.

5. Students will write words or phrases for each category on the chart to describe how they would write essays on their chosen topics differently for each audience. For example, this is a sample chart for the topic *Why I Like P.E.:*

peers	teachers	family members	other grownups	younger students/ siblings
I get to play games with my friends. This is a personal essay.	*P.E. lets us move around and then we can pay attention better in class.* This could be a compare/ contrast or persuasive essay.	*P.E. is the best part of my school day because I get to be outside.* This could be a descriptive or definition essay.	*P.E. is important. Kids learn to play new games and how to get along together.* This essay might focus on facts and information or cause and effect.	*Even if you don't like a game they play, you can have fun with your friends.* This essay could give personal perspectives or explain how to participate.

6. Explain that students will then develop that idea with details and examples as they write paragraphs or essays focused for that particular audience.

Closing

1. Have students think of a particular person from one category and write a paragraph or essay on their chosen topic with that audience in mind.

2. Encourage students to have that person read the paragraph and evaluate how well the student addressed the interests of the target audience.

Find a Purpose

Objective

Students will be given purposes for writing essays, and then use game cards to create a reference chart and write paragraphs.

Materials

- "Essay Cartoons," page 10
- chart from "Know Your Audience" lesson, page 18
- "Who? Why? What?" game cards, page 20
- cardstock
- blank cards, two per student

Preparation

Photocopy "Who? Why? What?" game cards onto cardstock, one set of cards per group of students. Have students cut cards apart.

Opening

1. List the purposes for writing essays on the board or display one set of purpose cards from the game cards.
2. Display cartoon figures from "An Essay for All Reasons" lesson.
3. Ask students which cartoon figure might go next to each purpose, or reason, to write that type of essay.
4. Ask students which types of essays might have more than one purpose. Rearrange cartoon figures to illustrate different reasons someone might write that type of essay.

Directions

1. Have students write possible essay topics on cards—two cards per student. Students will add their topic cards to their group's deck of game cards.
2. Divide students into groups of three or four students each. Give each group a deck of game cards.
3. Students will play a card game similar to "Go Fish." Each student receives five cards. Place remaining cards facedown in a pile. Students may draw from the facedown pile, the discard pile, or ask another player to obtain cards they need. The object is to make a set of cards consisting of one What? (essay type) card, one Why? (purpose) card, one Who? (audience) card, and one Topic card. The first player to make an *appropriate* set (that makes sense) wins. Suggest that play continue until each player has formed a set of cards.
4. Have students use their game card sets and the other game card sets in their group to create a chart for reference.

Closing

1. Have students use the set they formed during the game to write a paragraph.
2. Students will trade papers with other group members. They will read the paragraphs that they are given and evaluate them to complete the following sentence frame:

   Name wrote this essay paragraph to *purpose*.

3. Have each student check his or her sentences with the author of the paragraph for accuracy.

Who? What? Why? Game Cards

Who? (Audience)	Why? (Purpose)	What? (Type of Essay)
Who? teacher	**Why?** persuade	**What?** compare/contrast
Who? someone in the community (coach, librarian, other grownup)	**Why?** share your opinion	**What?** personal
Who? parents grandparents aunts/uncles	**Why?** make people think	**What?** cause and effect
Who? friends	**Why?** to describe	**What?** factual/informative
Who? classmates	**Why?** to show someone how to do something	**What?** process
Who? students in other classes pen pals	**Why?** present information	**What?** descriptive
Who? siblings cousins	**Why?** to entertain	**What?** persuasive

Search Out the Facts

Objective

Students will gather facts about an essay topic and write sample sentences.

Materials

- "Fact and Opinion Statements," page 22, for teacher reference
- sample "Fact File" cards, page 22, for class display
- cardstock or poster board, interactive whiteboard, or overhead projector and appropriate markers
- Research materials such as books, magazines, targeted Internet resources, etc. for students to research essay topics

Preparation

Enlarge sample Fact File cards for class display, photocopy on to overhead transparency, or scan into interactive whiteboard.

Opening

1. Review "Fact and Opinion Statements" with the class.
2. Have students use hand signals (for instance, using American Sign Language) to indicate whether each statement is a fact or an opinion.
3. Ask students for which types of essays a writer would want to include facts. (*Each type could include facts, details, and examples.*)
4. Ask students how they will find facts for their essays. (*research*)

Directions

1. Discuss what students can look for as they gather facts and information about an essay topic. (*who, what, where, when, why, how*)
2. Assign a topic from current studies or have students complete the sentence below to identify an essay topic.
   I would like to learn more about _____.
3. Display one or more sample "Fact File" cards.
4. Explain that using note cards like this will help students to use original sentences when they write. If they write key words and facts, it is easier to write in their own words instead of copying from the book. Explain the importance of writing in your own words. (*Plagiarism is against the law.*)
5. Have students use research materials to research their topics and create their own fact file cards.

Closing

1. Have students use their fact file cards to write sample sentences as follows.
   - a sentence with one or more details about the topic
   - an example or explanation about the topic
   - an unusual or especially interesting fact about the topic
2. You may wish to have students keep their fact file cards and sample sentences to use in a subsequent lesson when writing a practice essay.

Fact and Opinion Statements

(for teacher reference)

The telephone is the best invention ever made. (*opinion*)

Evaporation enables people to stay cool in the summer. (*fact*)

Death Valley is below sea level. (*fact*)

The Pacific Ocean is beautiful. (*opinion*)

The Amazon rain forest is in South America. (*fact*)

I think global warming is the reason it didn't freeze this January. (*opinion*)

Some people believe we get warts from frogs. (*opinion*)

Fact File Cards

Sea Lion

They live off the rocky coast of western North America.
Their range is from temperate coastal waters to the subpolar region.
Sea lions can swim up to 25 mph but move slowly on land.
Large groups of sea lions on land are called colonies.
Small groups in the water are called rafts.
Predators: killer whales (orcas), some sharks, humans
Diet: fish and squid, octopi, crabs, clams
Sea lions use their flat back teeth to crush shells.
They don't chew, they swallow large chunks of food.
Behavior: They often make barking or honking sounds.
They are intelligent, social, and playful, with a good sense of balance.
Sea lions adapt readily to captivity.

Snow Owl

They live year round on the Arctic tundra.
If food sources are scarce, they may migrate to Greenland or islands in Canada.
Snow owls have good night vision and long-range vision.
They can hunt day or night if necessary; in the summer, it doesn't get dark in the Arctic.
They hunt and fly silently.
Their alarm call sounds like quacking.
Diet: lemmings, hare, vole, shrews
Snow owls eat their food whole and spit pellets of bones and fur back out.
Breeding: They nest on the ground or on hummocks. (There are few trees in the far north.)
The mother stays on the nest, and the father brings food and protects her.
Owlets hatch in five weeks.
Both parents feed the owlets.

Make an Outline

Objective

Students will participate in an interactive experience, discover how to outline an essay, and then create practice outlines of their own.

Materials

- "Outline Cards," page 24, one set for class use
- cardstock
- "Sample Outline Illustration," page 25, for teacher reference
- whiteboard or overhead transparency and appropriate markers (optional)
- "Explorers Sample Outline," page 26, for teacher reference

Preparation

1. Enlarge and photocopy "Outline Cards" onto cardstock for students to hold.
2. Clear a space in the front or center of the room in which students can arrange themselves to demonstrate an outline.
3. Enlarge a copy of the sample outline illustration for display, if desired.

Opening

1. Distribute outline cards randomly, one per student. (Not all students will receive a card.)
2. Challenge students to arrange themselves in sequential order by going to the front of the room and standing in order. If students have trouble, refer to the sample outline illustration.

Directions

1. Copy the outline form onto a whiteboard or overhead transparency, or display prepared copy.
2. As a class, create a sample outline. You may wish to use a topic of current study. Refer to the sample outline, if necessary.
3. Once you have identified a topic, begin by asking students for main ideas for that topic (two or three).
4. Write a word or phrase for each idea.
5. Under each main idea, have students identify subtopics, or points they would like to make. (This is the A, B, C level.)
6. For the third level (1, 2, 3) have students list specific details, facts, and examples they could include about the subtopic.
7. Discuss the concept that students can organize subtopics (A, B, C level) in an essay in chronological or sequential order, in order of emphasis or importance, or moving from general to the specific.
8. Give each student index cards or pieces of paper. Assign students topics. You may wish to use units or chapters from a textbook, for instance science or social studies.

Closing

Have students work with partners to create outlines for their assigned topics.

Outline Cards

I.	**I.** 　**A.**	**I.** 　**A.** 　　**1.**	**I.** 　**A.** 　　**2.**	**I.** 　**A.** 　　**3.**	**I.** 　**B.**
I. 　**B.** 　　**1.**	**I.** 　**B.** 　　**2.**	**I.** 　**B.** 　　**3.**	**II.**	**II.** 　**A.**	**II.** 　**A.** 　　**1.**
II. 　**A.** 　　**2.**	**II.** 　**A.** 　　**3.**	**II.** 　**B.**	**II.** 　**B.** 　　**1.**	**II.** 　**B.** 　　**2.**	**II.** 　**B.** 　　**3.**
III.	**III.** 　**A.**	**III.** 　**A.** 　　**1.**	**III.** 　**A.** 　　**2.**	**III.** 　**B.**	**III.** 　**B.** 　　**1.**
III. 　**B.** 　　**2.**	**III.** 　**B.** 　　**3.**	**III.** 　**C.**	**III.** 　**C.** 　　**1.**	**III.** 　**C.** 　　**2.**	**III.** 　**C.** 　　**3.**

Sample Outline Illustration

Explorers Sample Outline

I. What did explorers accomplish?

    A. They claimed land for their country

    B. They discovered new lands

    C. They made maps

        1. example: Lewis & Clark

        2. example: Amerigo Vespucci

II. How did they travel?

    A. boat

    B. land

III. Why did they explore?

    A. to discover new land

        1. natural resources

        2. to claim land for their country

    B. riches

        1. trading

        2. conquer cities

Main Ideas and Details

Objective

Students will identify the main ideas and examples from a completed essay, and reconstruct the essay in a way that makes sense.

Materials

- "A Favorite Place," page 28, sample essay (reading level 4.2), one copy per student
- colored pencils, three different colors per student
- glue (optional)
- plain drawing paper, one piece per student (optional)

Preparation

Photocopy the sample essay and cut into strips at dotted lines.

Opening

1. Demonstrate a word association activity. Write a word that might be a common topic for student essays, such as *family*, a *beach*, or *baseball*, on the board or overhead transparency.

2. Read the word aloud. Tell the class you are going to write the first word that comes to your mind when you hear that word. For example, read aloud the word *beach*. Write *waves*. Read aloud *waves*. Write *water*. Read aloud *water*. Write *swim*. Ask a volunteer for a new word to write on the board. Call on students one at a time to give a new word for the ladder. Move quickly from one student to the next to allow brainstorming and fresh ideas.

3. Consider having students add words to an interactive whiteboard or take turns coming up and actually writing their words on the board or transparency. This will slow the process but allow for greater student participation and might help in groups with special needs or English language learners. Go through the process more than once if possible.

Directions

1. Ask students to review the principles of writing an essay from an outline. (*identify main points and sub-topic points; include facts, details, and examples*)

2. Tell students they will receive sentence strips from a sample essay. They will identify the main points and sub-points to reassemble the essay in an order that makes sense. You may wish to have them glue the strips in order on a separate piece of plain paper.

3. Once students have reassembled the essay, have them use colored pencils to mark facts, details, and examples, using a different color for each. Have students make a key somewhere on their paper identifying which color they use for facts, details, and examples.

Closing

1. Have students write a specific word on a slip of paper. Put all the papers into an "idea hat." Each student will draw out a word and use that word to start a new word ladder of his or her own.

2. Students will use the word lists they create to write a brief descriptive essay including facts, details, and examples.

A Favorite Place

(Sample Essay For Teacher Reference)

> **facts**
>
> *details*
>
> <u>examples</u>

One of my favorite places is a place that never looks the same. Our family goes to the ocean every year. We find many interesting things to do while we are there.

I like to watch the ocean waves crash against the rocks. **The surf is always changing. The sand on the beach looks different each time, too.** Sometimes **the wind has blown the sand into ridges.** *One time I saw large dunes and the next time the beach looked mostly flat.* **The wind and the waves wear away the rocks.** <u>If I took a picture with my camera each year, I might be able to see the weathering of the rocks.</u>

One thing I enjoy about our beach trips is having time with family. *We have time to just be together and talk.* <u>We sip hot cocoa or roast marshmallows at a campfire. One year another family gave us some fresh crab to try.</u> It tasted good on salad.

My family likes to explore rocks and tide pools together. We walk on the beach or build sand castles. If the water is warm enough, I love to play in the waves.

Every beach has something different to enjoy. A beach can have interesting rocks and places to hike, great crashing waves, or warm sand and water to swim in. Since it's never quite the same at the ocean, I can go back to my favorite place again and again.

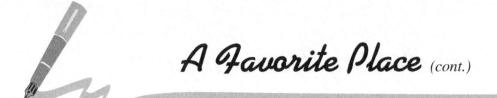

A Favorite Place (cont.)

One of my favorite places is a place that never looks the same.

Our family goes to the ocean every year.

We find many interesting things to do while we are there.

I like to watch the ocean waves crash against the rocks.

The surf is always changing.

The sand on the beach looks different each time, too.

Sometimes the wind has blown the sand into ridges.

One time I saw large dunes and the next time the beach looked mostly flat.

The wind and the waves wear away the rocks.

If I took a picture with my camera each year, I might be able to see the weathering of the rocks.

One thing I enjoy about our beach trips is having time with family.

We have time to just be together and talk.

We sip hot cocoa or roast marshmallows at a campfire.

One year another family gave us some fresh crab to try. It tasted good on salad.

My family likes to explore rocks and tide pools together.

We walk on the beach or build sand castles.

If the water is warm enough, I love to play in the waves.

Every beach has something different to enjoy.

A beach can have interesting rocks and places to hike, great crashing waves, or warm sand and water to swim in.

Since it's never quite the same at the ocean, I can go back to my favorite place again and again.

Introducing Your Topic

Objective
Students will practice writing an introductory paragraph for a topic.

Materials
- dress-up clothes suitable for an "explorer," such as cargo pants with pockets, backpack, canteen, hat, button-up jacket-type shirt that can be worn open
- "Explorers Sample Outline," page 26
- whiteboard or overhead projector and appropriate markers

Preparation
Have a student or guest from outside the class dress up as an explorer.

Opening
1. Introduce the "explorer" volunteer to the class. Be sure to include, for example:
- who this person is (*explorer*)
- why you want to introduce this person (*we all like to discover new things*)
- what you want to say about explorers (*sum up in one general sentence; refer to two or three main ideas the person writing the essay could write about*)
2. Ask students what you did to help them meet this new person. (*introduced him or her*)
3. Explain that an essay needs an introduction, the first paragraph of the essay, to introduce the topic to the reader.

Directions
1. Model how to write an introductory paragraph. Begin by asking students what they could say to grab their reader's attention. (*They could start with a question, such as "What is an explorer?", or provide an interesting fact.*)
2. Ask for suggestions for a second sentence that says something about the topic, related generally to one or more of the subtopics, for example, "An explorer is a person who wants to explore new places." (*discover new land*)
3. Remind students that an introduction may also contain one or more sentences that address a purpose related to the topic. (*people like to discover new things*)
4. Ask students to volunteer a sentence that indicates to the reader what the essay will be about. (*how explorers traveled, their reasons for exploring, etc.*)
5. Use one or more sentences to introduce all of the subtopics the essay will discuss.
6. Tell the class that the final sentence in this paragraph can sum up the topic, state the purpose of the essay, or it may lead into the first body paragraph. For example, explorers traveled for a variety of reasons and accomplished many different things.

Introducing Your Topic *(cont.)*

Closing

1. Have students use the outlines they created in the "Make an Outline" lesson or a chapter outline from a textbook to write a sample introductory paragraph.

2. Have students trade paragraphs with partners. They should not give their partners the outline they used for reference.

3. Students will recreate simple outlines from their partners' sample paragraphs.

4. Have students compare recreated outlines with the original outlines to evaluate how effectively the paragraphs introduced the topics.

Body Paragraphs

Objective

Students will practice writing detail sentences related to a particular main idea.

Materials

- index cards
- "Support for an Idea," pages 33 and 34, sample ideas and details
- container

Preparation

- Modify samples as needed to align with content with which your students are familiar.
- Prepare a card for each idea/detail set.
- In order to ensure each student has a card during the lesson, make multiple copies of the cards as needed.

Opening

1. Engage students in a question and answer game. Divide the class into two teams.
2. Explain that you will read details, one at a time. If the students on a team think they can state the main idea related to the details, they should raise their hands.
3. If the students guess the main idea before you have read all the related details, that team receives a point.
4. Direct the next set of details to the other team.
5. If a team cannot guess the main idea before you read all the details, allow the other team to guess and pick up the point before moving on to the next set of details.
6. Place all the cards in a container when you have finished playing the game.

Directions

1. Ask students to describe what types of information they would include in a body paragraph. (*details*, *facts*, *examples*) Explain the concept of examples and facts as needed.
2. Have students draw cards from the container.
3. Students will use their own words to write paragraphs using the main idea and details on the cards they drew from the container.

Closing

1. Collect student paragraphs and idea cards.
2. Read sample student paragraphs aloud, one paragraph at a time. Have students identify the main idea.

Support for an Idea

The Importance of Forests (main idea)
details:
They give oxygen back to the atmosphere.
They hold topsoil in place.
They prevent erosion.
They provide a home for plants and animals.
They release nutrients back into soil.

Learn How to Recycle (main idea)
details:
Find out what recycling programs your community has.
Put each category of recyclable items in a different place.
Set out your recycling for collection at the right time.
Take your recyclable items to a recycling facility.
Think before you throw anything away.

The Impact of the Steam Engine (main idea)
details:
They were invented to help get coal out of mines.
Steam engines were developed for railroads.
They transported goods.
Steam engines were adapted for passenger railways and boats.
They transported people.

Support for an Idea (cont.)

Bicycle Safety (main idea)

details:

Wear a bike helmet.

Helmets protect against head injury.

Make sure your helmet fits properly and meets safety standards.

Wear the helmet correctly.

Add reflective stickers to make it easier for drivers to see you.

Penguins Are Birds (main idea)

details:

Penguins don't fly, they swim.

Penguins lay eggs.

Penguin chicks have fluffy feathers.

Penguins use their wings for swimming.

Penguins waddle when they walk.

Penguins have many feathers, which helps them keep warm in frigid winters.

The Difference Between Butterflies and Moths (main idea)

details:

Butterflies have thin antennae that have a knob at the end.

Moths have feathery antennae with no knob at the end.

Moths have stout, hairy bodies.

Butterflies have slender abdomens.

The scales on moths' wings are larger.

Most butterflies fly during the day.

Most moths fly at night.

They often look the same at first glance.

They both have scales on their wings.

They have the same life cycle.

My Conclusion

Objective

Students will evaluate effective conclusions for an essay.

Materials

- "Conclusion Checklist," below, bulleted list for class use
- poster board or chart paper, and appropriate markers
- "Sample Conclusions," page 36, one copy per student
- index cards, one per group
- "Forests," page 37, sample essay, at least one copy per group (Reading Level 4.8)
- colored pencils or crayons
- plain white drawing paper, one piece per student

Preparation

1. List one point from the bulleted list, "Conclusion Checklist," on each card.
2. Each group will receive a card with one strategy listed on it.

Opening

1. Ask students to think about what they might include in the conclusion or last paragraph of an essay. Have them jot their ideas down on a piece of paper. Pair students with partners to discuss their ideas.
2. Call on student pairs to share their ideas with the class.

Directions

Part 1

1. As a class, create a conclusion checklist similar to the one below on chart paper or poster board.

Conclusion Checklist

☐ Sum up the main points.

☐ Provide a final perspective on the topic.

☐ Describe your feelings about the topic.

☐ Tell a short story (anecdote).

☐ State a decision or realization you have come to based on the facts in the essay.

☐ Answer the question "so what?" related to the essay.

☐ Show how the main points of the essay all fit together like a puzzle.

☐ Show readers how to use or apply the information in the essay to the "real world."

My Conclusion (cont.)

Directions (cont.)

2. Display the class-generated checklist so all students can refer to it, or make a copy available for student use.

3. Distribute copies of the "Sample Conclusions" paragraphs. Have students work with the same partners to evaluate the effectiveness of each conclusion. Students can do this by checking which characteristics listed on the conclusion chart they notice in each sample paragraph.

Part 2

1. Divide students into groups. Give each group an index card with a conclusion strategy written on it.

2. Distribute copies of the sample essay to group members. Each group will write a concluding paragraph for the essay using the strategy listed on their card.

Closing

1. Have all students think about the sample essay and draw mental pictures to help them visualize the topic and main ideas of the essay. You may wish to have students draw actual pictures of their mental images.

2. Ask students how drawing a picture might help them to write a conclusion for the essay. Use any concepts from the bulleted list that apply.

Sample Conclusions

Chimpanzees (by S.R.)

Now you know more about chimps. You know what they eat, where they live, and how old they can be. Maybe you could go to Africa and study them someday. (sums up the main point)

Finding and Eating Wild, Edible Plants (by A.R.)

Let's imagine again. You're lost in a forest, and you notice a small plant. You easily identify it, and nibble a small section to test. You make a small fire and cook it, and you're full of energy and food when the Search and Rescue find you! (shows the reader how to apply the information)

Caleb (by K.M.)

Without a word, Caleb and I shook out our sandy memories and salty tears next to the pump. Back home, we finished our homework. Then we went to sleep. When the sun rose the next day, our adventures seemed a distant memory. (sums up main points, relates feelings about the topic)

Forests

Temperate forests have warm, wet summers and cool, rainy winters. Most trees in these forests lose their leaves. The leaves change color in the fall. Many plants grow in the fertile soil. Mammals, birds, reptiles, insects, and spiders live in these forests. Small animals move about in the heavy undergrowth. You can probably think of many animals that live in a temperate forest.

An evergreen forest is cool and dry. Coniferous trees, or trees that have cones, grow there. The soil is dry and rocky. Not as many plants grow on the ground in these forests. Many mammals, birds, insects, and spiders also live in these forests.

Thick evergreen forests grow along the western coastline of the United States. The slopes of the Cascade Mountains are also covered with forests.

The east and west sides of the Cascades do not have the same climate. They also have different natural plants. The forests of the western slopes are thick. Mosses, ferns, and bushes grow beneath the trees. Hemlocks, firs, and cedar trees grow in the damp marine forests of the western Cascades.

The eastern slopes get much less rain and the forests are not as thick. Not as many plants grow on the forest floor. The most important tree of the eastern forests is the Ponderosa pine.

Thick forests cover much of the land along the coast. This wet and mild climate is very good for trees. A special kind of forest, called a *rain forest*, is found on the Olympic Peninsula. It is thick, green, and full of many kinds of plants.

The tropical rain forest is warm and very wet. Even though the soil may be thin, many fascinating plants and animals live in the rain forest. Most of the animals live high up in the trees, where there is more sunlight and rain. Thousands of smaller creatures live on the forest floor, in the leaves, twigs, and rotten wood that have fallen to the ground.

Making Sense of Essays

Objective

Students will contribute to a class essay and evaluate transitions.

Materials

- container (to hold topic questions)
- interactive whiteboard or overhead projector and appropriate markers
- "Conclusion Checklist" (class-generated chart or bulleted list from "My Conclusion" lesson), one copy per group

Note: this lesson may take more than one class period.

Opening

1. Invite each student to write a question about a topic that might make a good subject for an essay.
2. Collect the papers and place them in a container. Pull a slip of paper from the container. If the question is appropriate, read it aloud to the class. (If it is not appropriate, pull out another question.)
3. Write the question on the board. As a class, identify a keyword that states the topic.

Directions

Part 1

1. Once the class has identified a topic, divide students into five groups. Assign each group one of the five senses: hearing, sight, smell, taste, and touch.
2. Have students write words and phrases describing the topic as it relates to their assigned sense.
3. Students will use these notes and work cooperatively to write a paragraph.

Part 2

1. When groups have completed their paragraphs, compile and scan them into an interactive whiteboard, photocopy them onto a transparency, or otherwise enlarge them for class display.
2. Work together as a class to place the paragraphs in an order that makes sense.
3. Use colored markers to identify key ideas that will help students write an introductory paragraph.
4. As a whole group, write an introduction for the essay.
5. Ask students to recall transition words. (*e.g., therefore, however, since, first, next, then, last, finally, etc.*)
6. Discuss which transition words and phrases could be added to make the essay read more smoothly.

Closing

1. Review concepts from "My Conclusion."
2. Regroup students as before. Have groups use the approach they think best to write a conclusion for the class essay.
3. Post or display group paragraphs anonymously or read aloud. Have students vote on the most effective conclusion.

Practice: Cause and Effect

Objective
Students will diagram causes and effects and write an essay

Materials
- arrow cards, two per group
- cardstock or heavy paper, half sheet size, three per group
- "Sample Cause-and-Effect Questions," page 41, one copy for class display
- interactive whiteboard or overhead projector and appropriate markers (optional)

Preparation
1. Photocopy and cut out arrows. (Student volunteers may cut out arrows prior to the lesson.)
2. Cut cardstock into half-sheet size.
3. Enlarge list of cause and effect questions for class display, scan into interactive whiteboard, or copy onto overhead transparency.

Opening
1. Ask a volunteer to suggest an event that recently happened in the classroom or at school, for example:

   The children played Narnia at recess.

2. Write the sentence describing the event on the board. Post an arrow before the sentence:

   ➡ **The children played Narnia at recess.**

3. In front of the arrow write the word "cause." Ask students what caused this event to happen. Why did students play Narnia at recess? (Several had just read the book or watched the movie.)

   cause ➡ **The children played Narnia at recess.**

4. Place an arrow card after the sentence. Write the word "effect" after the arrow.

   cause ➡ **The children played Narnia at recess.** ➡ **effect**

5. Ask students what happened as a result of playing Narnia at recess. (More kids in the class played together, they understood the story better, more people wanted to read the book.)

Directions

Part 1
1. Divide students into groups of four to six students each. Give each group three pieces of cardstock and two arrow cut-outs.
2. Post the prepared list of suggested cause and effect questions. Have each group choose a question and write it on a piece of cardstock in large letters.

Practice: Cause and Effect *(cont.)*

Directions *(cont.)*

3. Group members will place the card with the question on the desk and then place an arrow card before the question.

4. On another piece of cardstock, students will write the word "Cause." Have students brainstorm reasons why this event or condition happens or what causes it. They should list the reasons on the card.

5. Have students place an arrow card after the question. On the third piece of card stock they will write the word "Effect." Students will brainstorm what happens as a result of this event or condition, or the consequences of the action, and list their responses on the card.

Part 2

1. Have groups present their cause-and-effect diagrams one group at a time to the class.

2. Group members will stand in front of the class, each holding a card in the proper sequence. One or more students may have to hold more than one card.

3. Have one person read the cause-and-effect scenario aloud.

Closing

1. Review with students how to write a cause and effect essay.

   • Include why something happens or what caused it to happen.

   • Explain what happens as a result of the event or condition.

   • Include an opening statement in the introductory paragraph.

   • Support your ideas with facts and examples.

   • Organize your essay so it makes sense.

   • Select an appropriate conclusion strategy, such as provide a final perspective on the topic, describe your feelings about the topic, state a decision or realization you have come to based on the facts, or show the reader how to use or apply the information in the essay.

2. Have students use the scenario they discussed with their group and write an individual cause and effect essay.

Sample Cause-and-Effect Questions

- Why would someone choose to play on a soccer team?
- What are the effects of TV on school work?
- Why do students misbehave at school?
- How does the computer affect your school work?
- Think of a favorite character in a book or movie. What caused that character's behavior? What were the results?
- How does pain affect someone's life?
- What causes a volcano to erupt?
- What is the effect of exercise on your health?
- Think of a choice you made last week. List the reasons you made that choice and what happened after you made that decision.
- If you stay up to watch a movie on Sunday night, what effects might you experience on Monday?
- What were the causes and effects of the pilgrim's voyage on the *Mayflower*?

Arrow Cards

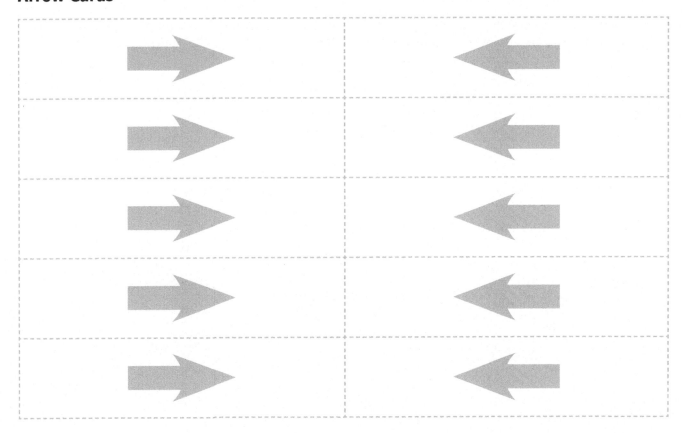

Practice: Compare and Contrast

Objective
Students will create Venn diagrams and write compare-and-contrast essays.

Materials
- pictures of a dog and a cat
- interactive whiteboard, or overhead projector and appropriate markers
- "Venn Diagram," page 44, one for each student
- "Compare and Contrast Topics," page 45, enough so that each student has one

Preparation
1. Scan a blank Venn diagram into an interactive whiteboard, photocopy onto overhead transparency, or enlarge for class display. (Use the provided diagram on page 44 or a template in Microsoft Word or interactive whiteboard software.)
2. Photocopy and cut apart the "Compare and Contrast Topics" cards.

Opening
1. Show the class the pictures of a dog and a cat.
2. Display the blank Venn diagram. Ask the students how these animals are similar and how they are different. Use the class discussion to complete the Venn diagram (see suggestions below).

Dogs   **Cats**

come when you call
often like to swim
greet you and lick your
    face
like to play in the yard
bark
like to go with you

Dogs and Cats

make good pets
have tails
both can be playful
both go to a vet for
    health care

like to take naps
do not like baths
do not always want to be
    petted
purr
would rather stay home

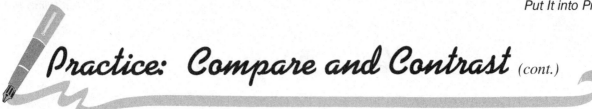

Practice: Compare and Contrast (cont.)

Directions

1. Review the concept of compare and contrast with students. Explain that in this type of essay, they will discuss how two things are similar and how they are different. As in other types of essays, it will be important to have facts, examples, and good organization of the essay.

2. Tell students they will need to introduce the two things they are comparing in the introductory paragraph. They can write one or two general sentences to set up the contrast between the two.

3. Provide students with a blank Venn diagram.

4. Randomly distribute one topic card to each student. Ask students to determine specific items to compare based on their topic suggestion.

5. Have students complete the Venn diagrams.

6. They will then exchange their papers with partners. Students will use different-colored pencils to add ideas in any or all categories of the Venn diagram. They will then return their partners' papers.

7. Have students write compare-and-contrast essays. Encourage them to incorporate their partners' ideas as well as their own from the Venn diagram.

Closing

1. Collect student essays. Redistribute so each student has a classmate's essay.

2. Ask students to write journal entries expressing which option they prefer based on the arguments set forth in the essays.

3. Allow students to read their classmate's journal responses to their compare-and-contrast essays.

Venn Diagram

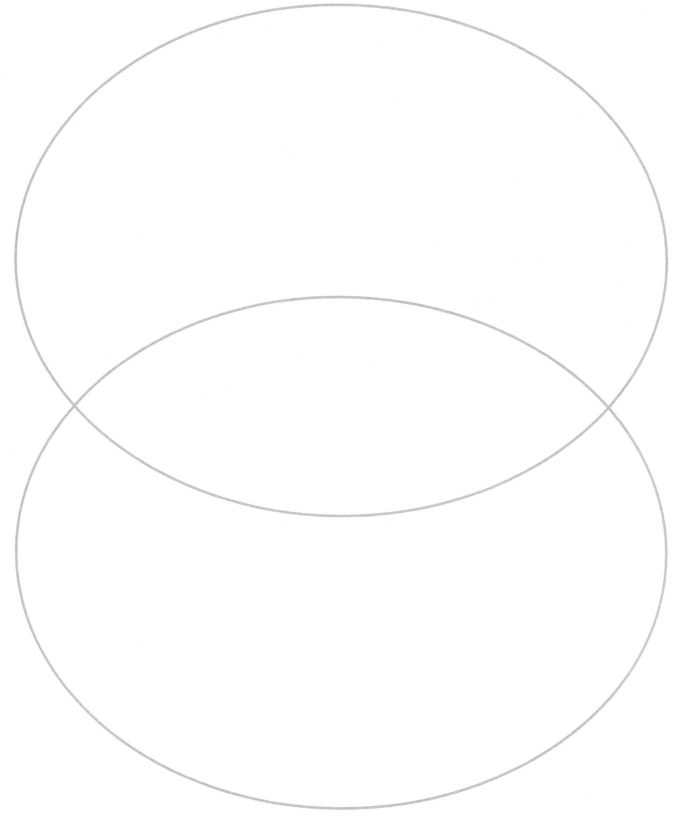

©Teacher Created Resources, Inc.

Compare-and-Contrast Topics

two of your favorite sports or games	a book and a movie of the same title	two different places you have visited
two of your favorite foods	two different pets, other than a dog and a cat	different purchase options (for example—two video game systems or two different bicycle models)
moving to a different school or neighborhood compared to staying in the same school or neighborhood	snow and rain or a hurricane and a blizzard	going to a movie or watching a movie at home
two fairy tales (for example—The Three Bears and The Three Little Pigs, or Red Riding Hood and Goldilocks)	two different types of shoes	two different forms of energy (for example, solar heat and wind power)

Practice: Response to Literature

Objective

Students will write responses to literature and respond to classmates.

Materials

- current literature story or book

Preparation

Select five or six students to be on the panel for the panel discussion.

Opening

1. Identify a topic of current interest in the classroom.
2. Have students write one or two questions about that topic.
3. Tell the class they will hear opinions expressed about the topic.
4. Conduct a panel discussion. Select a few student questions and ask the panel to respond verbally.

Directions

1. Refer to the opinions expressed during the panel discussion. Ask students how they think the panel members felt about the topic. How could they tell?
2. Help students identify words or phrases that expressed emotions or opinions.
3. Briefly discuss the concept of responding in writing to something a student has read. For example, when we read a letter and respond to it, we answer any questions, tell how or what we are doing, ask questions, and respond to the other person by expressing feelings or experiences.
4. Explain that students can do the same things when responding to literature. They can try to answer any questions they had while reading the selection, write what they will remember about the piece and why, pose questions and ideas related to the reading, and express their feelings or personal experiences related to the content of the selection.
5. Have students write their own responses to the literature selection. Encourage them to express feelings and opinions, but remind them also to use examples and details from the story, as well, to support their statements.
6. Allow time for students to write a one- or two-page essay that includes an introduction, two or three main points in body paragraphs, and a conclusion.

Closing

1. Randomly redistribute student essays so that students can read a classmate's essay.
2. Have students identify feelings and opinions expressed in the essay and complete the following sentence frames.

   ___(classmate)___ thinks that ___(title of story)___ is ___(opinion or feeling)___ .

   ___(classmate)___ feels ___(opinion or feeling)___ about ___(title of story)___ .

Editing and Preparing to Publish

Objective

Students will label specific aspects they should check when editing their own writing.

Materials

- sample student essays or one of the samples provided in a previous lesson, one copy for display and one copy per student
- poster board and appropriate markers (optional)
- Directions from "Introducing Your Topic" lesson, page 30
- "Conclusion Checklist", page 35
- student essays completed in prior lessons, one per student
- examples of published essays

Preparation

1. Prepare an anonymous sample essay by labeling specific aspects with numbers or letters. For example—label any grammar, punctuation, or spelling errors with separate numbers. Label paragraph indentations and margins. Place a number by the title, or where a title should be, and next to the introduction and conclusion.

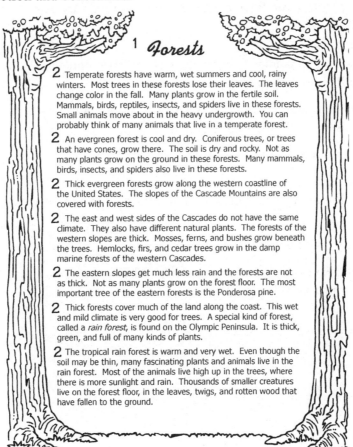

1 **Forests**

2 Temperate forests have warm, wet summers and cool, rainy winters. Most trees in these forests lose their leaves. The leaves change color in the fall. Many plants grow in the fertile soil. Mammals, birds, reptiles, insects, and spiders live in these forests. Small animals move about in the heavy undergrowth. You can probably think of many animals that live in a temperate forest.

2 An evergreen forest is cool and dry. Coniferous trees, or trees that have cones, grow there. The soil is dry and rocky. Not as many plants grow on the ground in these forests. Many mammals, birds, insects, and spiders also live in these forests.

2 Thick evergreen forests grow along the western coastline of the United States. The slopes of the Cascade Mountains are also covered with forests.

2 The east and west sides of the Cascades do not have the same climate. They also have different natural plants. The forests of the western slopes are thick. Mosses, ferns, and bushes grow beneath the trees. Hemlocks, firs, and cedar trees grow in the damp marine forests of the western Cascades.

2 The eastern slopes get much less rain and the forests are not as thick. Not as many plants grow on the forest floor. The most important tree of the eastern forests is the Ponderosa pine.

2 Thick forests cover much of the land along the coast. This wet and mild climate is very good for trees. A special kind of forest, called a *rain forest*, is found on the Olympic Peninsula. It is thick, green, and full of many kinds of plants.

2 The tropical rain forest is warm and very wet. Even though the soil may be thin, many fascinating plants and animals live in the rain forest. Most of the animals live high up in the trees, where there is more sunlight and rain. Thousands of smaller creatures live on the forest floor, in the leaves, twigs, and rotten wood that have fallen to the ground.

Editing and Preparing to Publish

Preparation *(cont.)*

2. Have students bring in samples of published essays, for instance, from children's magazines, newspapers, textbook inserts, etc.

Opening

1. Display the sample prepared essay. Distribute copies to each student.

2. Have students identify the purpose and any corrections needed for each label. Work together as a class to edit the essay, or have students make corrections on their own.

Directions

1. Refer to the sample edited essay to further discuss the process of editing. Students may already be familiar with the concept of checking grammar, spelling, and punctuation but may not have much practice checking for paragraph indentation and clear margins.

2. Review the concepts from "Introducing My Topic" and "Conclusion Checklist" about how to write an effective introduction and a conclusion for an essay.

3. Make sure that each student has a copy of an essay he or she has written to edit.

4. Ask students to use the displayed sample to guide them through editing each aspect of their essays.

5. Allow time for students to write final, corrected copies of their essays.

Closing

1. Ask students to share the examples of published essays they collected. Discuss various ways in which students could publish their essays.

- Suggest that students consider creating a book of essays about their state for inclusion in the school library, community library, or community center.

- Propose that students write letters to the editor of a local newspaper.

- Have students compile essays on a topic of community interest, such as a local festival or holiday, into a brochure for distribution through the local library or community center.

- Have students practice their problem-solving and persuasive-writing skills by writing essays suggesting ways they could help improve your school.

- Ask students to write essays about wellness and healthy habits as part of a health unit. They can create a magazine or brochure for local clinics.

48

©*Teacher Created Resources, Inc.*